play	stray	way	may
take	shake	space	bake
brain	pain	paint	wait
sight	tight	bright	might
spice	rise	pride	mile
sly	try	why	my

Busy Beaver Builders

 Identifying prefixes: *un-, re-*

 Identifying prefixes: *pre-, mis-*

Materials:
supply of the recording sheet on page 12
center mat on page 13
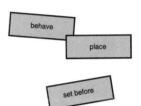
○ prefix, word, and meaning cards on page 15
○ prefix, word, and meaning cards on page 17
2 resealable plastic bags

Preparing the centers:
1. Laminate the center mat and cards if desired.
2. Cut out the cards and put each set into a separate bag.
3. Place the bags, center mat, and copies of the recording sheet at a center.

Using the centers:
1. A student removes the cards from the bag.
2. She places the prefix cards on the center mat where indicated.
3. She builds a word by selecting a word card and placing it beside the correct prefix.
4. She finds the meaning card for the new word and lays it on the center mat.
5. She copies the word and its meaning in the corresponding sections of the recording sheet.
6. She removes the word cards and meaning cards from the mat.
7. She continues in this same manner with the remaining word cards.

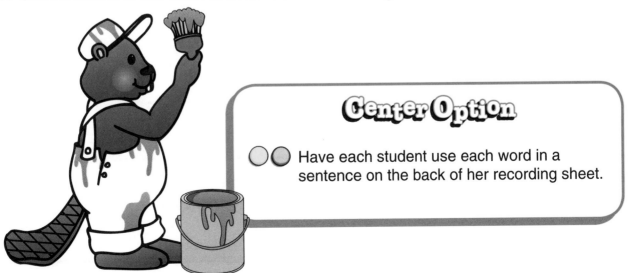

Center Option
○○ Have each student use each word in a sentence on the back of her recording sheet.

Busy Beaver Builders

Color the circle to match the back of your word cards. ◯

Write the word you made and its meaning below.
Remove the word cards and meaning cards from the mat.
Continue in this same manner with the remaining cards.

Word	Meaning

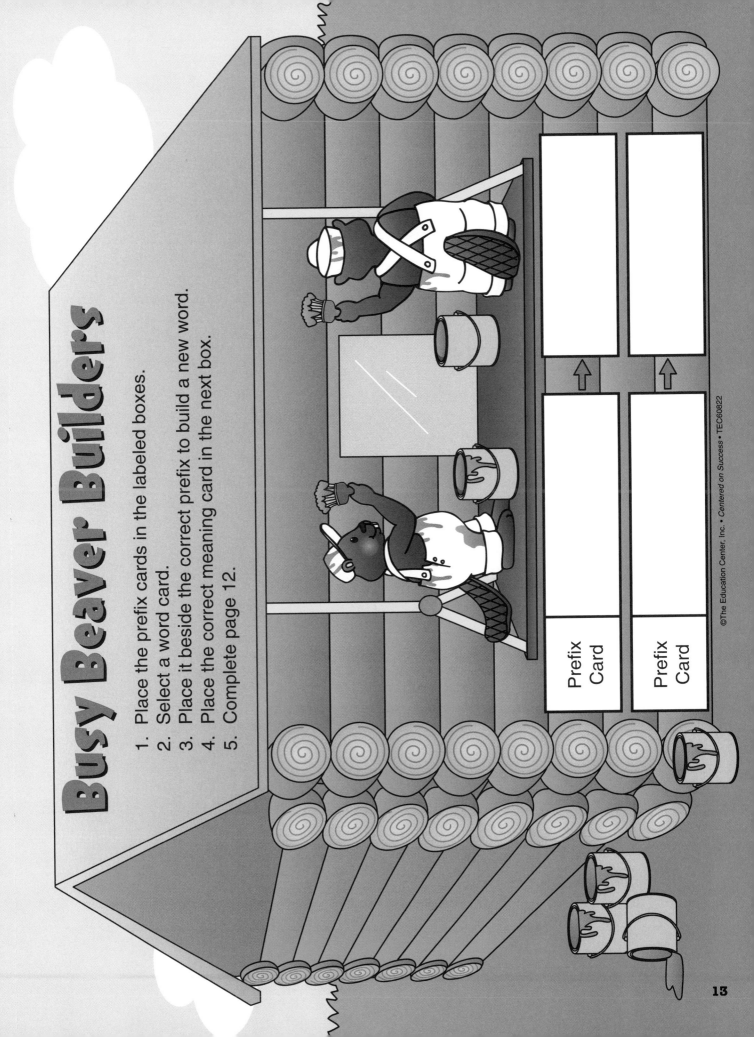

Busy Beaver Builders

1. Place the prefix cards in the labeled boxes.
2. Select a word card.
3. Place it beside the correct prefix to build a new word.
4. Place the correct meaning card in the next box.
5. Complete page 12.

Prefix Card

Prefix Card

14

fair	happy	test
draw	true	write
prepared	try	sure
read	not fair	not prepared
not true	not sure	not happy
write again	read again	test again
try again		
draw again		

un	re

pay	match	treat
view	spell	heat
place	behave	set
wash	behave poorly	mix up
spell incorrectly	treat poorly	to lose
wash before	set before	heat before

pay before
view before

pre	mis

Having a Ball!

 Identifying suffixes: *-ful, -ly*

 Identifying suffixes: *-er, -est*

Materials:

supply of the recording sheet on page 20
center mat on page 21
sentence cards and suffix balls on page 23
sentence cards and suffix balls on page 25
2 resealable plastic bags

Preparing the centers:

1. Laminate the center mat, sentence cards, and suffix balls if desired.
2. Cut out the cards and balls. Put each set into a separate bag.
3. Place the bags, center mat, and copies of the recording sheet at a center.

Using the centers:

1. A student removes the sentence cards and suffix balls from the bag.
2. He places the suffix balls on the circles where indicated.
3. He places card 1 on the mat and moves each suffix ball, in turn, onto the card to help him determine which suffix correctly completes the word.
4. He writes the sentence on his recording sheet.
5. He returns the balls to the top of the center mat and continues in this same manner with the remaining cards.

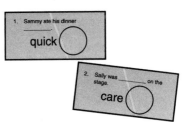

Center Option

Invite pairs to complete the center together by taking turns moving the suffix balls to correctly complete each word. Provide a copy of the answer key for students to check each other's answers.

Name _____

Having a Ball!

Color the circle to match the back of your ◯ center cards.

Write sentence 1 on the line provided.
Return the balls to the top of the center mat.
Continue in this same manner with the
   remaining cards.

1. _____

2. _____

3. _____

4. _____

5. _____

6. _____

7. _____

8. _____

9. _____

10. _____

Note to the teacher: Use with the directions on page 19.

Having a Ball!

1. Place a suffix ball on each circle.
2. Order the cards and stack them faceup beside the mat, with card 1 on top.
3. Place card 1 on the sidewalk and read the sentence.
4. Use the suffix balls to help you decide on the missing suffix.
5. Complete page 20.

Place card here.

1. Sammy ate his dinner _____.

   quick ◯

2. Sally was _____ on the stage.

   care ◯

3. The seals rested _____ after dinner.

   quiet ◯

4. Scott hit the ball _____ to Sammy.

   soft ◯

5. Eating fish makes the seals _____.

   cheer ◯

6. Sally and Scott are very _____ after lunch.

   play ◯

7. The seals' mother tries to be _____.

   help ◯

8. All the seals swim _____ after they eat.

   slow ◯

9. Sammy likes to play with _____ balls.

   color ◯

10. The seals wait _____ for their dinner each night.

    calm ◯

1. Sally is _____ in the sun than in the water.

   warm ◯

2. Of all the seals, Sammy is the _____.

   loud ◯

3. Scott's teeth are the _____ in the family.

   clean ◯

4. Scott is _____ than Sally.

   old ◯

5. The seals think they are the _____ animals.

   smart ◯

6. Sally's ball is _____ than Sammy's.

   new ◯

7. The seals' mother's stage is the _____.

   tall ◯

8. Sally's flippers are _____ than Scott's.

   short ◯

9. Sammy can balance a ball _____ than Sally.

   long ◯

10. Juggling five balls is _____ than juggling three.

    hard ◯

Open Up!

 Identifying simple main ideas and supporting details

 Identifying more complex main ideas and supporting details

Materials:

supply of the recording sheet on page 28
center mat on page 29
○ door and doormat cards on page 31
◑ door and doormat cards on page 33
2 resealable plastic bags

Preparing the centers:

1. Laminate the center mat and cards if desired.
2. Cut apart the cards and put each set in a separate bag.
3. Place the bags, center mat, and copies of the recording sheet at a center.

Using the centers:

1. A student removes the cards from the bag.
2. She lays the door cards in order on the center mat.
3. She reads the list on door 1 and decides on the main idea.
4. She places the matching main idea doormat under the door.
5. She continues in this same manner with the remaining door cards and then completes the recording sheet on page 28.

Center Option

○ ◑ Invite the student to draw several doors and doormats on the back of her recording sheet. Challenge her to program them with additional supporting details and main ideas.

Open Up!

Color the circle to match the back of your door cards. ⚪

Copy the words from the center mat onto each door.
Write the main idea on each doormat.

Note to the teacher: Use with the directions on page 27.

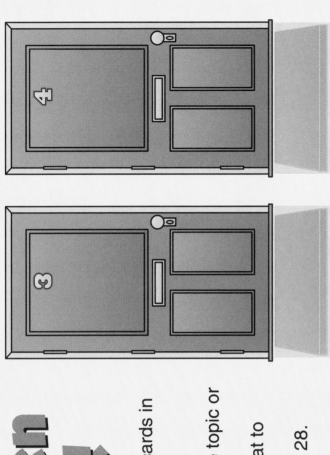

Open Up!

1. Lay your door cards in order.
2. Read each list.
3. Think about the topic or main idea.
4. Match a doormat to each door.
5. Complete page 28.

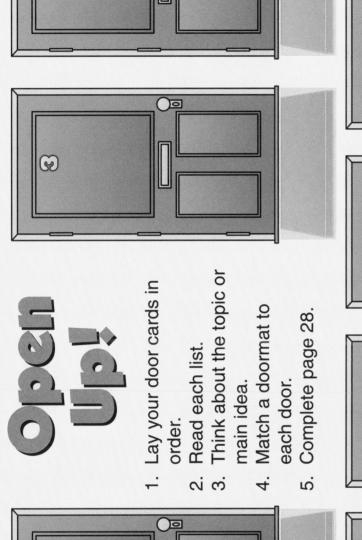

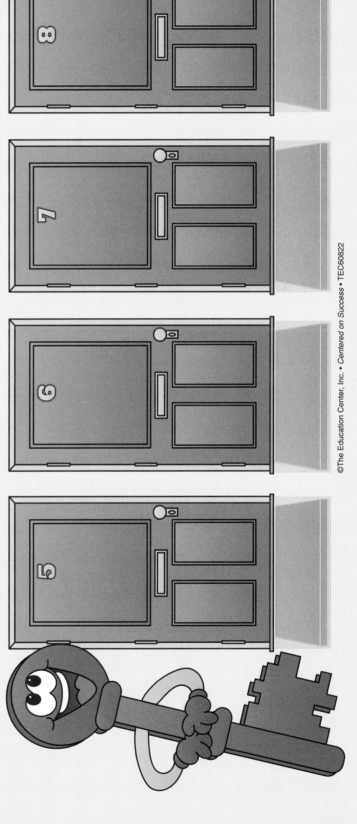

©The Education Center, Inc. • Centered on Success • TEC60822

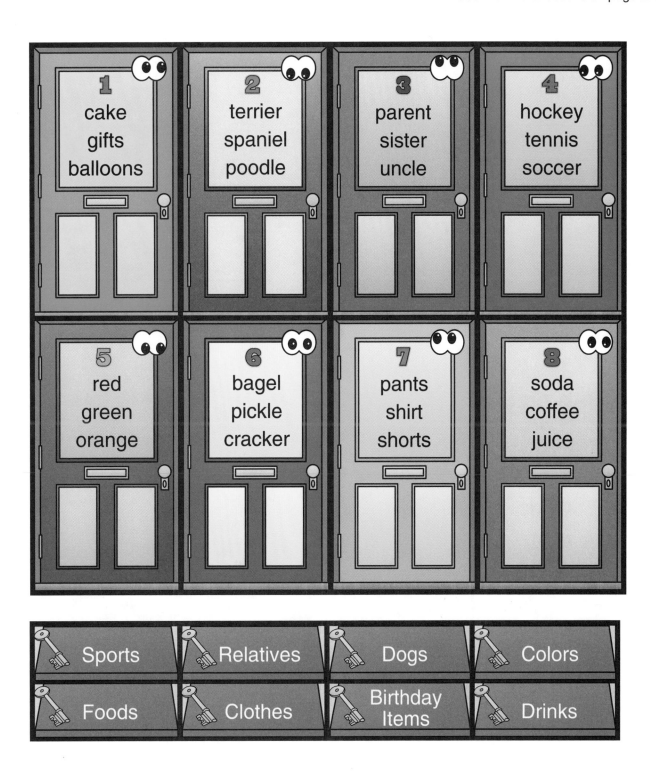

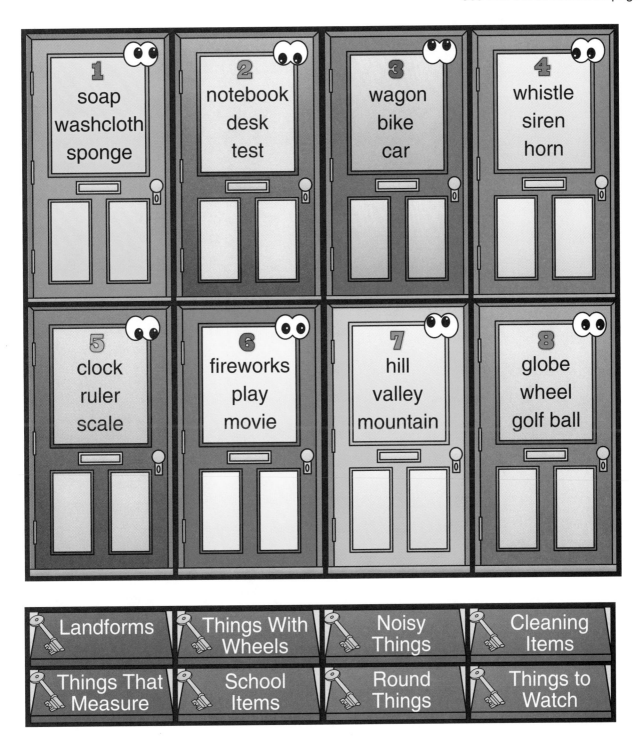

1. soap washcloth sponge
2. notebook desk test
3. wagon bike car
4. whistle siren horn
5. clock ruler scale
6. fireworks play movie
7. hill valley mountain
8. globe wheel golf ball

Landforms

Things With Wheels

Noisy Things

Cleaning Items

Things That Measure

School Items

Round Things

Things to Watch

Is That a Fact?

 Identifying simple facts and opinions

 Identifying more complex facts and opinions

Materials:
supply of the recording sheet on page 36
center mat on page 37
center crayons on page 39
center crayons on page 41
2 resealable plastic bags

Preparing the centers:
1. Laminate the center mat and crayons.
2. Cut out the crayons and put each programmed set into a separate bag.
3. Cut slits in the center mat where indicated.
4. Place the bags, center mat, and copies of the recording sheet at a center.

Using the centers:
1. A student removes the crayons from the bag.
2. He selects a crayon and reads the sentence.
3. He decides if the sentence is a fact or an opinion.
4. He places the crayon in the correct crayon box.
5. He continues in this same manner with the remaining crayons.
6. He completes the recording sheet on page 36.

Center Options

Provide two empty crayon boxes labeled similarly to those on the center mat. Have students place the crayons in these boxes.

Program the open crayons with additional sentences.

Name _____

Is That a Fact?

Color the circle to match the back of your center crayons. ◯

Remove the crayons from the "Facts" crayon box.
Copy the sentences below.

Facts

_____

_____

_____

_____

Remove the crayons from the "Opinions" crayon box.
Copy the sentences below.

Opinions

_____

_____

_____

_____

©The Education Center, Inc. • *Centered on Success* • TEC60822 • Key p. 163

36 **Note to the teacher:** Use with the directions on page 35.

Is That a Fact?

Opinions

Facts

1. Read each sentence.
2. Place each crayon in the correct box.
3. Complete page 36.

37

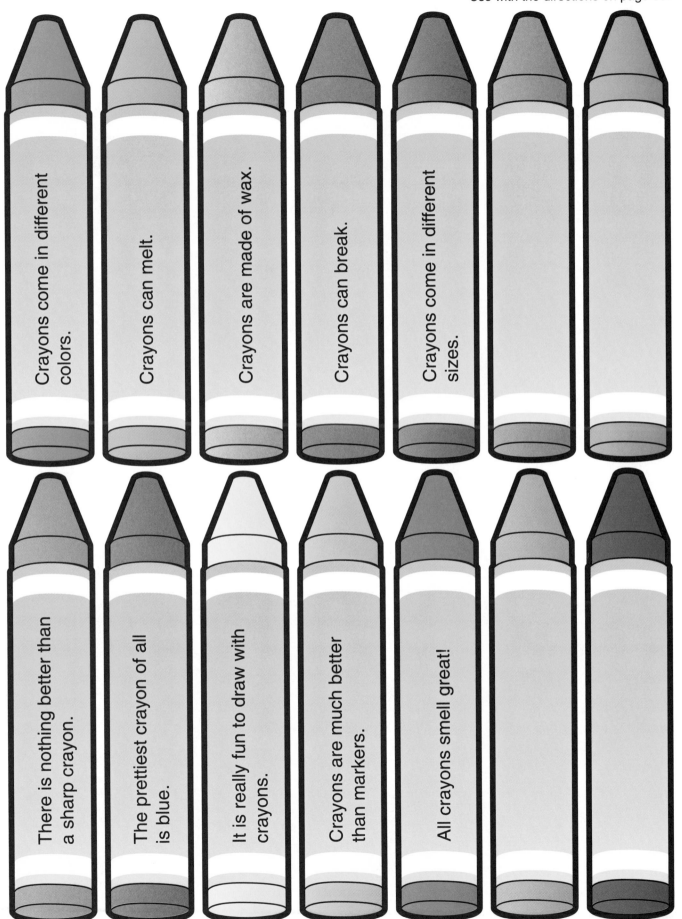

Crayons come in different colors.

Crayons can melt.

Crayons are made of wax.

Crayons can break.

Crayons come in different sizes.

There is nothing better than a sharp crayon.

The prettiest crayon of all is blue.

It is really fun to draw with crayons.

Crayons are much better than markers.

All crayons smell great!

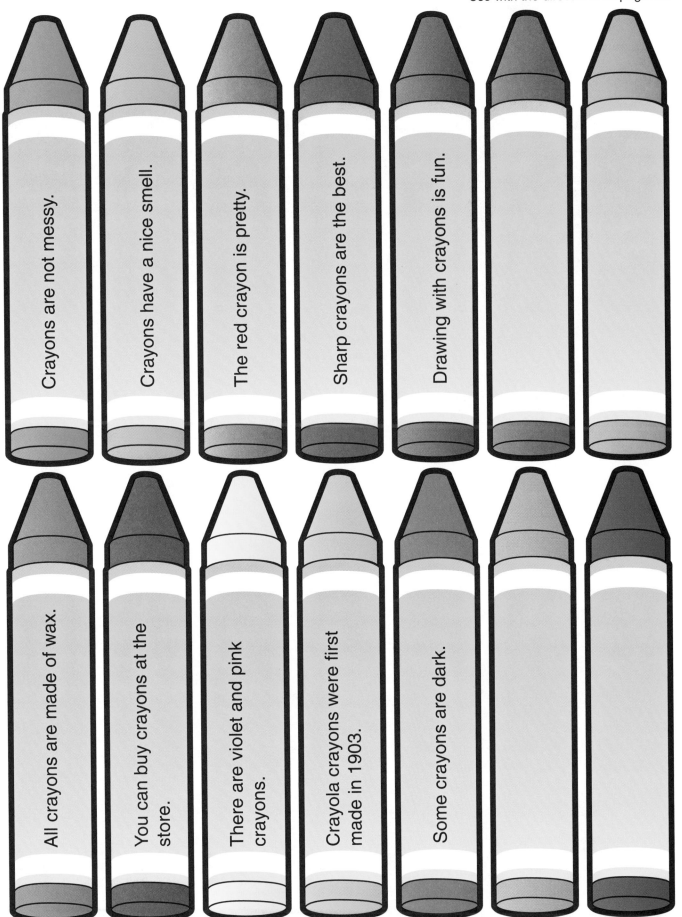

Crayons are not messy.

Crayons have a nice smell.

The red crayon is pretty.

Sharp crayons are the best.

Drawing with crayons is fun.

All crayons are made of wax.

You can buy crayons at the store.

There are violet and pink crayons.

Crayola crayons were first made in 1903.

Some crayons are dark.

Put It There, Partner!

 Using capitalization and ending punctuation marks (period, question mark)

 Using capitalization and ending punctuation marks (period, question mark, exclamation point)

Materials:

supply of the recording sheet on page 44
center mat on page 45
tumbleweed cards on page 47
tumbleweed cards on page 49
2 resealable plastic bags

Preparing the centers:

1. Laminate the center mat and cards if desired.
2. Cut out the cards. Put each programmed set into a separate bag.
3. Place the bags, center mat, and copies of the recording sheet at a center.

Using the centers:

1. A student removes the cards from the bag and stacks them in order with card 1 on top.
2. She chooses card 1 and reads it.
3. If the sentence has correct punctuation, she places it in the left lasso on the center mat.
4. If the sentence has incorrect punctuation, she places it in the right lasso.
5. She continues in this same manner with the remaining cards.
6. She completes the recording sheet on page 44.

Center Option

 Program the open tumbleweed cards with additional sentences with correct and incorrect punctuation marks.

43

Name ____________________ *Using capitalization and ending punctuation marks*

Put It There, Partner!

Color the circle to match the back of your tumbleweed cards. ○

Gather the incorrect cards from the right lasso on the center mat.
Write the sentences on the lines below, adding the correct punctuation.

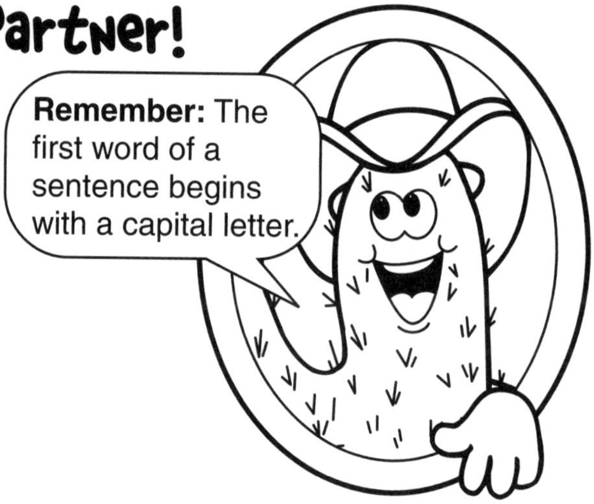

Remember: The first word of a sentence begins with a capital letter.

1. ______________________________

____

2. ______________________________

____

3. ______________________________

____

4. ______________________________

____

5. ______________________________

____

6. ______________________________

____

7. ______________________________

____

8. ______________________________

____

Note to the teacher: Use with the directions on page 43.

Put It There, Partner!

Correct

Incorrect

1. Choose a tumbleweed card and read it.
2. If the punctuation is correct, place it in the left lasso.
3. If the punctuation is incorrect, place it in the right lasso.
4. Continue in this same manner with the remaining cards.
5. Complete page 44.

is this a large desert.	How does a cactus survive in the desert?	This desert is sandy.	a cactus can store its own water?
why does a cactus have sharp spines.	We went on vacation to the desert.	many different kinds of animals live in the desert?	the desert can get very cold at night?
How hot does it get in the desert?	there is not much water in the desert?	Is the desert flat or hilly.	I would like to have a cactus of my own?

I had a cactus? do you know where it is!	Temperatures in the desert can reach 107°F wow, that's really hot.	Many animals live in the desert. What do they eat?	Can you grow your own cactus how do you do it!
You can see wolves in the desert. There's one right now!	I'd like to visit the desert someday when can we go.	Wow, this is beautiful. it reminds me of home?	There are many spiders living in the desert? Some are very large?
Look! It's a baby lizard!	This desert is very flat? Do you know where we are!	Would you like to visit the desert someday! sure.	A cactus has pointy spines. Sometimes they can hurt you.

Ant Antics

 Using commas: dates, locations

 Using commas: locations, items in a series

Materials:

supply of the recording sheet on page 52
center mat on page 53
○ sentence strips on page 55
○ sentence strips on page 57

Preparing the centers:

1. Laminate the center mat and strips.
2. Cut out the strips.
3. Cut slits in the center mat where indicated.
4. Place the programmed strips, center mat, and copies of the recording sheet at a center.

Using the centers:

1. A student inserts the strip into the slits in the center mat.
2. He slides the strip down to show sentence 1.
3. He copies the sentence correctly on the recording sheet on page 52, adding commas where needed.
4. He continues in this same manner with the remaining sentences.

Center Options

○ ○ Store the sentence strips in a clean, empty potato chip container.

○ ○ Program the open strips with additional sentences.

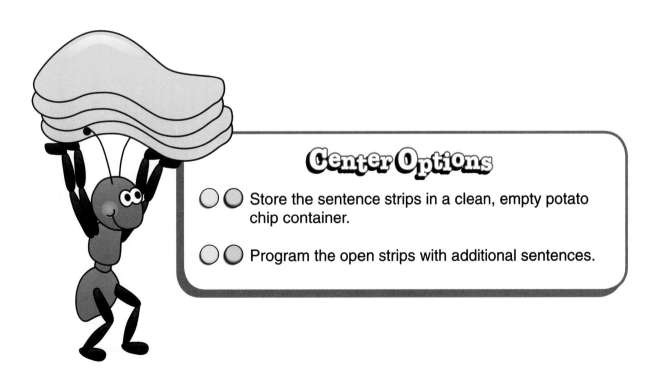

Ant Antics

Color the circle to match the back of your sentence strip. ◯

Copy sentence 1 from the strip on the line below.
Add commas where needed.
Continue in the same manner with the remaining
   sentences.

1. _____

2. _____

3. _____

4. _____

5. _____

6. _____

7. _____

8. _____

9. _____

10. _____

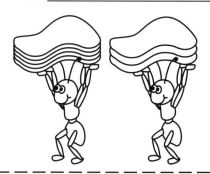   

Ant Antics

Tater Crisps

1. Insert the strip into the slits.
2. Slide the strip to show sentence 1.
3. Complete page 52.

_____

_____

10. Ada was born on March 26 2001.	10.
9. Annie lives in Spokane Washington.	9.
8. The Ant family reunion was June 15 2003.	8.
7. Ada and Annie went to a picnic on July 4 2002.	7.
6. Ada Ant moved to Miami Florida last year.	6.
5. Alex Ant was born on September 23 2000.	5.
4. Annie started Ant School on August 28 1999.	4.
3. The Ant family lives in Richmond Virginia.	3.
2. Annie Ant visited Lincoln Nebraska last month.	2.
1. The Ants went to the beach on May 29 2002.	1.

10. Alex lives in Atlanta Georgia.

9. Annie bought ice cream milk and bread at the store.

8. Ada bought pants shoes and socks for the trip.

7. The Ant family visited Raleigh North Carolina.

6. The museum is in Santa Fe New Mexico.

5. Ada Ant needed paper pencils and glue for school.

4. The world's largest picnic is in Chicago Illinois.

3. Alex Ant took a train to Sacramento California.

2. The Ants might move to Detroit Michigan.

1. Annie Ant loves pizza potato chips and chocolate.

10.

9.

8.

7.

6.

5.

4.

3.

2.

1.

Catching a Web of Words

 Identifying and capitalizing proper nouns: days, months, holidays

 Identifying and capitalizing proper nouns: places, locations

Materials:
supply of the recording sheet on page 60
center mat on page 61
⬤ fly cards on page 63
⬤ fly cards on page 65
2 resealable plastic bags

Preparing the centers:
1. Laminate the center mat and cards if desired.
2. Cut out the cards and put each programmed set in a separate bag.
3. Place the bags, center mat, and copies of the recording sheet at a center.

Using the centers:
1. A student removes the cards from the bag.
2. She selects a fly card and reads the word or phrase.
3. If the word or phrase is a proper noun, she places the card on the web.
4. If the word or phrase is not a proper noun, she places the card in the discard pile.
5. She continues in this same manner with the remaining cards.
6. She completes the recording sheet on page 60.

Center Option
⬤⬤ Program the open fly cards with additional words or phrases.

Name _____

Catching a Web of Words

Color the circle to match your center cards. ◯

Correctly write each proper noun in a box.

Remember:
A proper noun begins with a capital letter.

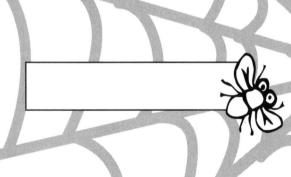

©The Education Center, Inc. • *Centered on Success* • TEC60822 • Key p. 164

Note to the teacher: Use with the directions on page 59.

Catching a Web of Words

Remember: A proper noun names a **special** person, place, or thing.

We're saved!

1. Help Spider catch flies by placing cards with proper nouns on the web.
2. Place cards with other nouns in the discard pile.
3. Complete page 60.

Discard Pile

party	monday	july	february
park	june	family	september
wednesday	kwanzaa	flag day	parade

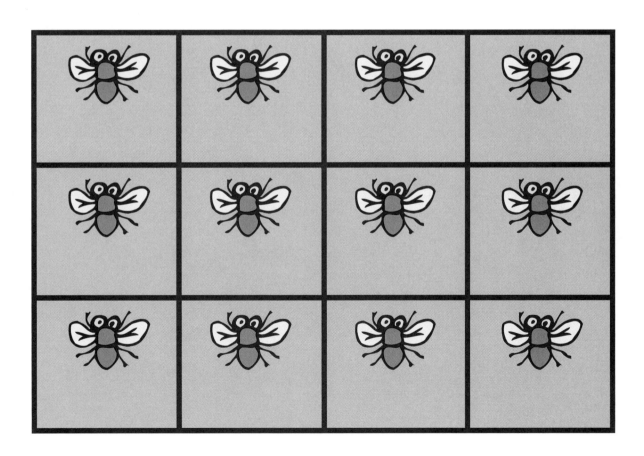

house	dover drive	ann's gift shop	state street
bramble bakery	restaurant	the happy hotel	taxicab
sugar creek	old village school	city	pine point park

What's the Scoop?

 Identifying contractions: *not, is*

 Identifying contractions: *not, have, will*

Materials:

supply of the recording sheet on page 68
center mat on page 69
ice-cream scoop and bowl cards on page 71
ice-cream scoop and bowl cards on page 73
2 resealable plastic bags

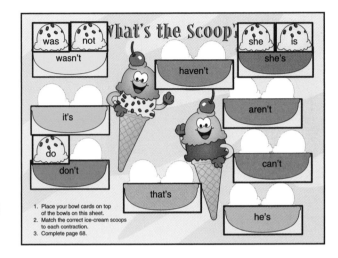

Preparing the centers:

1. Laminate the center mat and cards if desired.
2. Cut out the cards and put each set into a separate bag.
3. Place the bags, center mat, and copies of the recording sheet at a center.

Using the centers:

1. A student removes the cards from the bag.
2. He reads the contraction on each bowl card and finds the corresponding words on the ice-cream scoop cards.
3. He places the matching ice-cream scoops and bowls on the center mat.
4. He completes the recording sheet on page 68.

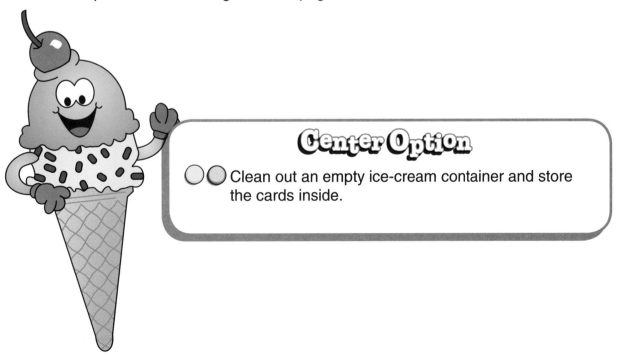

Center Option

Clean out an empty ice-cream container and store the cards inside.

What's the Scoop?

Color the circle to match the back of your center cards. ◯

Label the ice-cream scoops and bowls to match your
   completed center mat.

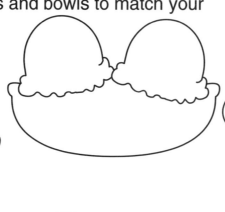

What's the Scoop?

1. Place your bowl cards on top of the bowls on this sheet.
2. Match the correct ice-cream scoops to each contraction.
3. Complete page 68.

©The Education Center, Inc. • *Centered on Success* • TEC60822

69

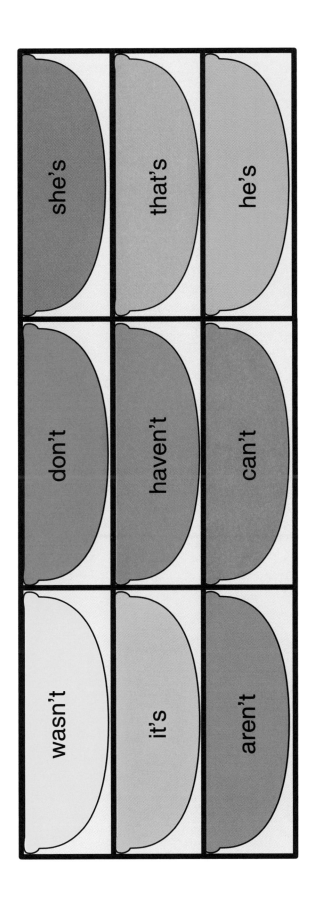

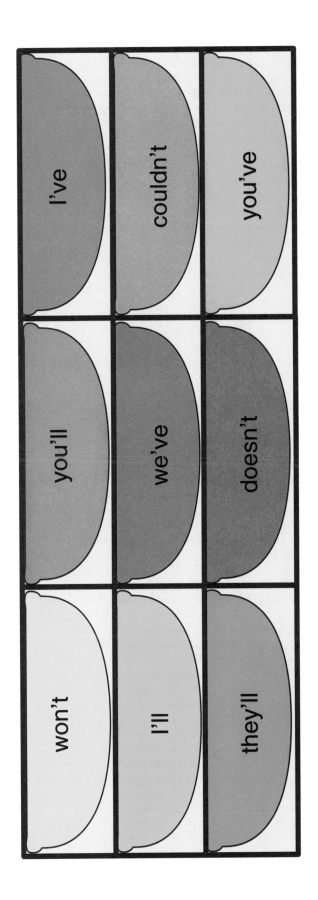

Pad Hoppin'

 Identifying parts of speech: nouns, verbs

 Identifying parts of speech: nouns, verbs, adjectives

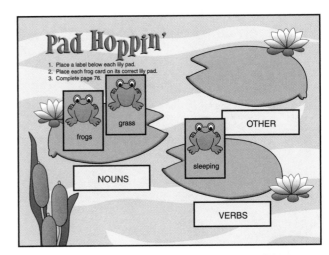

Materials:
supply of the recording sheet on page 76
center mat on page 77
frog cards and labels on page 79
frog cards and labels on page 81
2 resealable plastic bags

Preparing the centers:
1. Laminate the center mat, frog cards, and labels if desired.
2. Cut out the cards and labels and put each programmed set in a separate bag.
3. Place the bags, center mat, and copies of the recording sheet at a center.

Using the centers:
1. A student removes the cards from the bag.
2. He places the labels on the center mat where indicated.
3. He reads the word on each frog card and places it on the appropriate lily pad.
4. He completes the recording sheet on page 76.

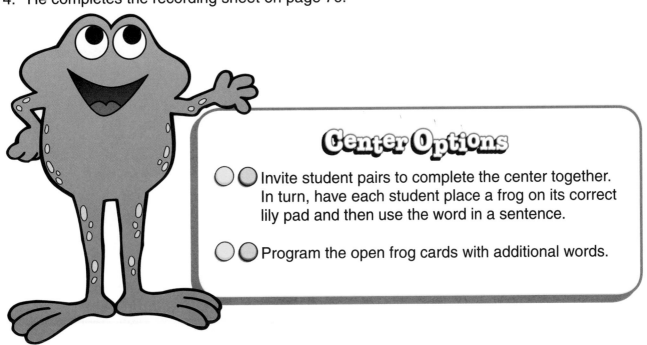

Center Options
Invite student pairs to complete the center together. In turn, have each student place a frog on its correct lily pad and then use the word in a sentence.

Program the open frog cards with additional words.

Name _____

Pad Hoppin'

Color the circle to match the back of your frog cards. ◯

Label the lily pads to match your center labels.
Write each word on the correct lily pad.

Note to the teacher: Use with the directions on page 75.

Pad Hoppin'

1. Place a label below each lily pad.
2. Place each frog card on its correct lily pad.
3. Complete page 76.

Place label here.

Place label here.

Place label here.

of	sleeping	frogs	wiggle
leaf	eat	legs	loudly
grass	the	sits	big

OTHER

VERBS

NOUNS

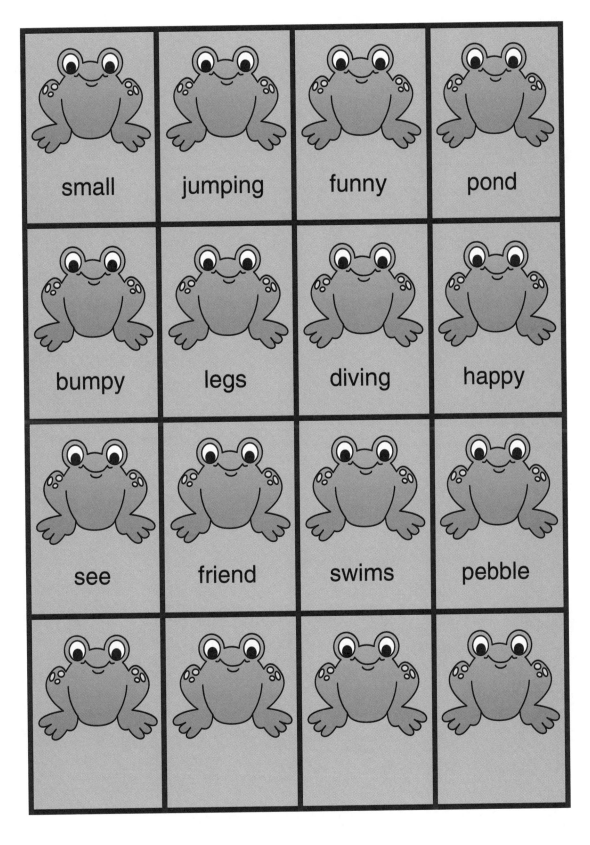

small

jumping

funny

pond

bumpy

legs

diving

happy

see

friend

swims

pebble

ADJECTIVES

VERBS

NOUNS

Quackers & Milk

 Comparing numbers to 1,000

 Comparing numbers to 10,000

Materials:
supply of the recording sheet on page 84
center mat on page 85
number strips on page 87
number strips on page 89

Preparing the centers:
1. Laminate the center mat and strips.
2. Cut out the strips.
3. Cut slits in the center mat where indicated.
4. Place the programmed strips, center mat, and copies of the recording sheet at a center.

Using the centers:
1. A student inserts the strip into the slits in the center mat.
2. She slides the strip to show problem A.
3. She writes the problem on the recording sheet on page 84 below its corresponding letter.
4. She writes the correct sign (< or >) on the duck's bill.
5. She continues in the same manner with the remaining problems.

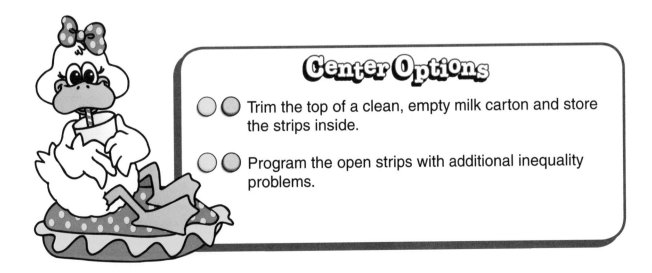

Center Options

Trim the top of a clean, empty milk carton and store the strips inside.

Program the open strips with additional inequality problems.

Quackers & Milk

Color the circle to match the back of your number strips. ◯

Copy problem A from the strip.
Write the correct < or > sign on the duck's bill.
Continue in this same manner with the remaining problems.

 A.
_____

 B.
_____

 C.
_____

 D.
_____

 E.
_____

 F.
_____

 G.
_____

 H.
_____

 I.
_____

 J.
_____

 K.
_____

 L.
_____

1. Insert the strip into the slits.
2. Slide the strip to show problem A.
3. Complete page 84.

Quackers & Milk

L.   633 ___ 631

K.   476 ___ 467

J.   546 ___ 564

I.   202 ___ 220

H.   301 ___ 310

G.   892 ___ 891

F.   764 ___ 674

E.   999 ___ 991

D.   961 ___ 691

C.   712 ___ 721

B.   301 ___ 299

A.   214 ___ 241

L.

K.

J.

I.

H.

G.

F.

E.

D.

C.

B.

A.

L.   8,000 ___ 8,888

K.   5,297 ___ 5,710

J.   9,212 ___ 9,121

I.   6,162 ___ 6,261

H.   8,500 ___ 8,150

G.   7,403 ___ 7,304

F.   1,358 ___ 1,357

E.   2,001 ___ 2,100

D.   5,425 ___ 4,525

C.   9,911 ___ 9,199

B.   6,350 ___ 6,560

A.   7,999 ___ 8,000

L.

K.

J.

I.

H.

G.

F.

E.

D.

C.

B.

A.

Ready, Set, Go!

 Multiplying basic facts: 1–4

 Multiplying basic facts: 1–6

Materials:
supply of the recording sheet on page 92
center mat on page 93
number wheels on page 95
number wheels on page 97
2 brads

Preparing the centers:
1. Laminate the center mat and wheels.
2. Cut out the wheels and the windows in the center mat where indicated.
3. Poke a small hole through the black dot on each wheel and on the center mat.
4. Place the programmed wheels, center mat, brads, and copies of the recording sheet at a center.

Using the centers:
1. A student uses a brad to attach each wheel to the back of the center mat.
2. He turns the left wheel to show problem A.
3. He turns the right wheel to show the answer to problem A .
4. He writes the problem and its answer on the recording sheet on page 92 beside its corresponding letter.
5. He continues in this same manner with the remaining problems.

Center Option
Program the open wheels with additional multiplication problems and answers.

Name_____

Ready, Set, Go!

Color the circle to match the back of your number
wheels. ◯

Copy problem A from the left wheel onto trophy A.
Copy the answer from the right wheel.
Continue in this same manner with the remaining problems.

A.   X ____

B.   X ____

C.   X ____

D.   X ____

E.   X ____

F.   X ____

G.   X ____

H.   X ____

I.   X ____

J.   X ____

K.   X ____

L.   X ____

   Note to the teacher: Use with the directions on page 91.

Ready, Set, Go!

1. Attach each number wheel to the back of this sheet with a brad.
2. Turn the left wheel so that problem A shows through the window.
3. Turn the right wheel so that the answer to problem A shows through the window.
4. Complete page 92.

Right Wheel

Cut out.

Left Wheel

Cut out.

7

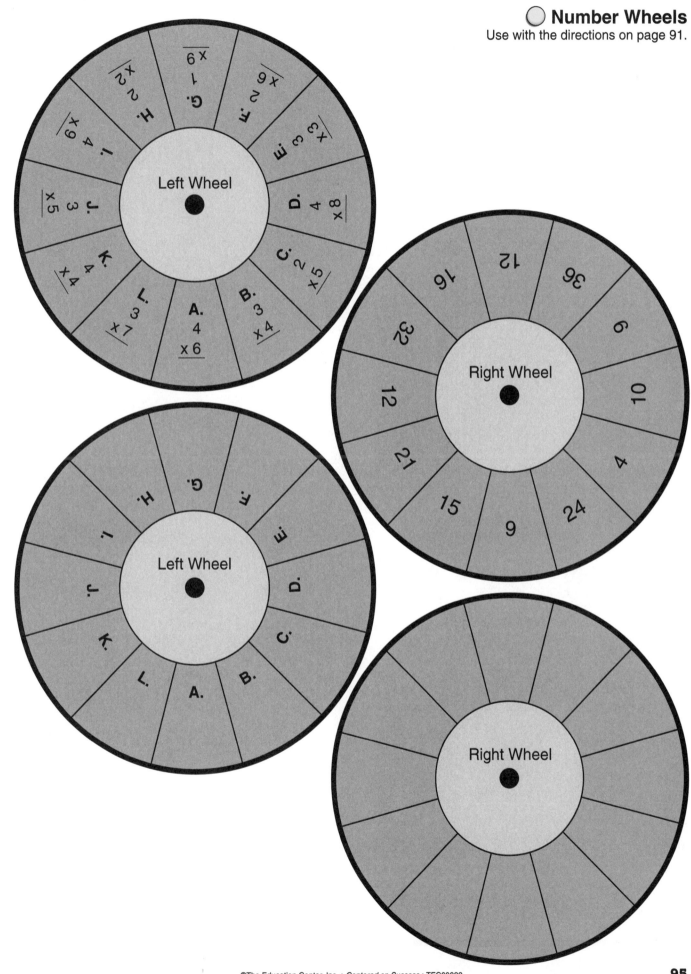

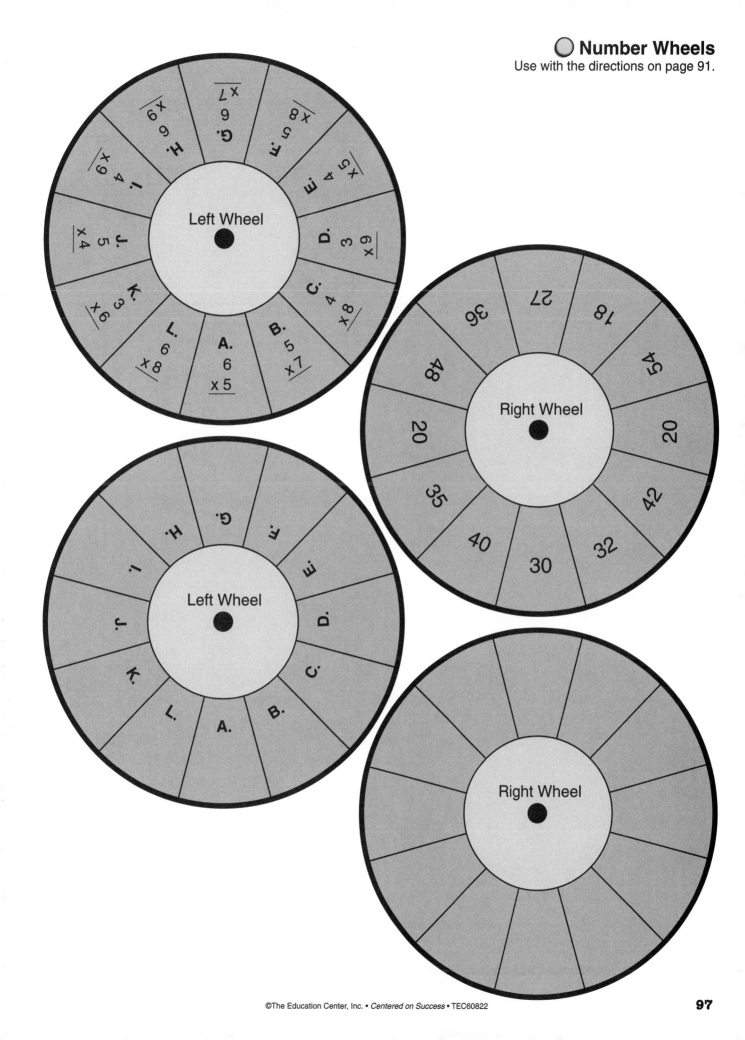

Left Wheel

A. 6 ×5
B. 5 ×7
C. 4 ×8
D. 6 ×3
E. 5 ×4
F. 5 ×8
G. 6 ×7
H. 6 ×9
I. 4 ×9
J. 5 ×4
K. 3 ×6
L. 6 ×8

Right Wheel

27, 36, 48, 20, 35, 40, 30, 32, 42, 20, 54, 18

Left Wheel

A. B. C. D. E. F. G. H. I. J. K. L.

Right Wheel

Mouse on the Moon

 Multiplying basic facts: 1–6

 Multiplying basic facts: 1–8

Materials:
supply of the recording sheet on page 100
center mat on page 101
○ number cards on page 103
○ number cards on page 105
2 resealable plastic bags
large paper clip
sharpened pencil

Preparing the centers:
1. Laminate the center mat and cards if desired.
2. Cut the cards apart and put each set into a separate bag.
3. Place the bags, center mat, sharpened pencil, paper clip, and copies of the recording sheet at a center.

Using the centers:
1. A student removes the number cards from the bag.
2. She chooses a card and places it on the center mat where indicated.
3. She uses the pencil and paper clip to make a spinner as shown.
4. She spins the paper clip and uses the number to complete the math sentence shown on the card.
5. She writes the math sentence on the recording sheet on page 100 and then solves the problem.
6. She continues in this same manner with the remaining cards.

Center Options

○ ○ For a star-studded decor, attach self-adhesive star stickers to the resealable plastic bags.

○ ○ After students successfully complete the center, present them with star-shaped awards titled "Congratulations on your bright work with multiplication!"

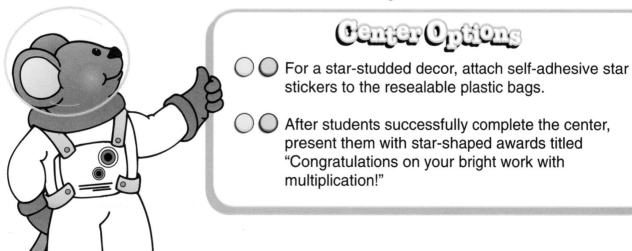

Mouse on the Moon

Color the circle to match the back of your number cards. ◯

Write the math sentence you made.
Write the answer.
Continue in this same manner with the remaining cards.

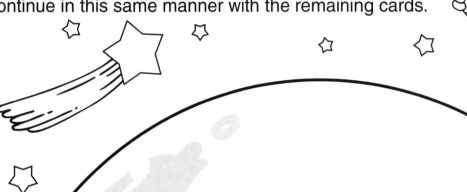

___ X ___ = ___   ___ X ___ = ___

___ X ___ = ___   ___ X ___ = ___

___ X ___ = ___   ___ X ___ = ___

___ X ___ = ___   ___ X ___ = ___

___ X ___ = ___   ___ X ___ = ___

___ X ___ = ___   ___ X ___ = ___

___ X ___ = ___   ___ X ___ = ___

Place card here.

Mouse on the Moon

1
2
0
3
9
4
8
5
7
6

1. Choose a card and place it on the center mat.
2. Use the pencil and paper clip to create a spinner.
3. Spin the paper clip and use the number to complete the math sentence.
4. Complete page 100.

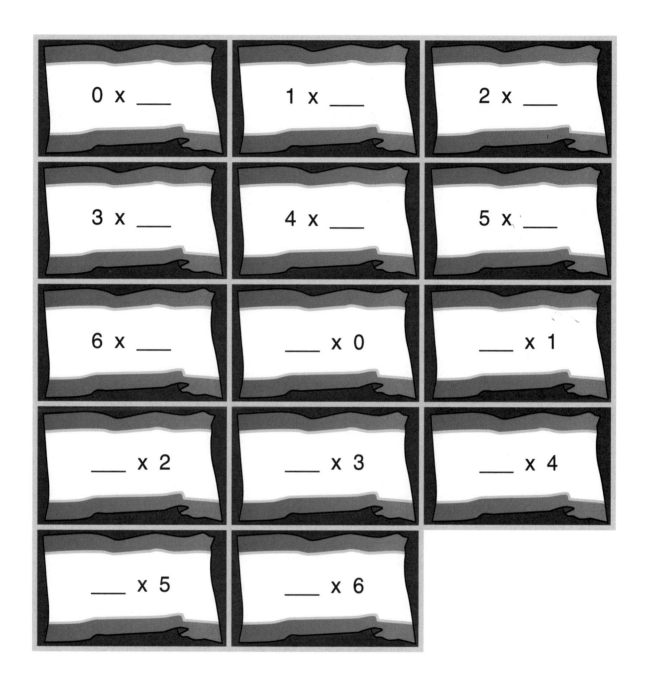

0 x ___

1 x ___

2 x ___

3 x ___

4 x ___

5 x ___

6 x ___

___ x 0

___ x 1

___ x 2

___ x 3

___ x 4

___ x 5

___ x 6

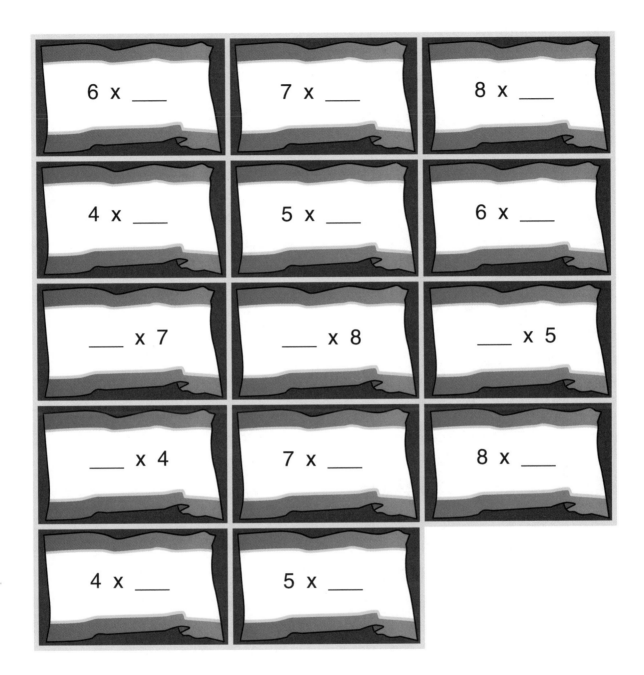

6 x ___

7 x ___

8 x ___

4 x ___

5 x ___

6 x ___

___ x 7

___ x 8

___ x 5

___ x 4

7 x ___

8 x ___

4 x ___

5 x ___

Slam Dunk Math!

 Multiplying basic facts: 1–8

 Multiplying basic facts: 1–10

Materials:

supply of the recording sheet on page 108
center mat on page 109
basketball cards on page 111
basketball cards on page 113
2 resealable plastic bags

Preparing the centers:

1. Laminate the center mat and cards if desired.
2. Cut apart the cards and put each set into a separate bag.
3. Place the bags, center mat, and copies of the recording sheet at a center.

Using the centers:

1. A student removes the cards from the bag and stacks them faceup near the center mat.
2. He selects a basketball card, reads the problem, and lays it on the hoop with the matching answer.
3. He continues in this same manner with the remaining cards.
4. He completes the recording sheet on page 108.

Air Tiger
1

Center Option

Invite pairs to complete the center together by taking turns placing basketball cards on their correct hoops. Provide an answer key for students to check each other's work.

Slam Dunk Math!

Color the circle to match the back of your basketball cards. ◯

Copy each fact and its answer below.

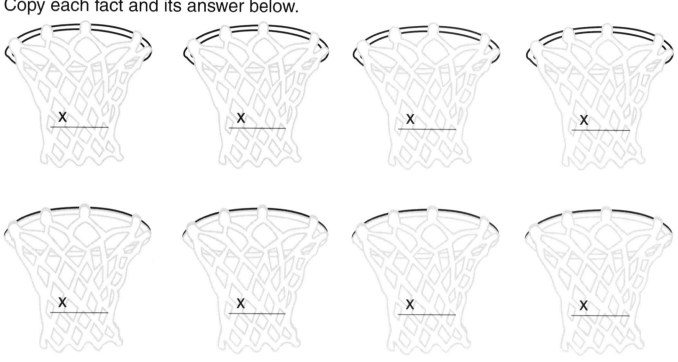

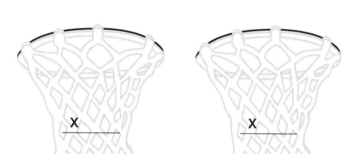

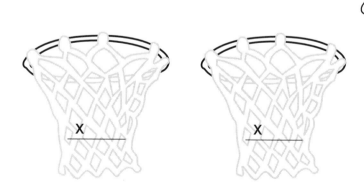

Slam Dunk Math!

48

64

45

54

72

18

63

56

24

32

49

27

20

35

90

70

50

80

15

36

30

81

60

1. Choose a basketball card and solve the math fact.
2. Lay the card on the hoop with the matching answer.
3. Complete page 108.

All Abuzz!

 Identifying multiplication and division fact families: 1–5

 Identifying multiplication and division fact families: 1–9

Materials:
supply of the recording sheet on page 116
center mat on page 117
⚪ number strips on page 119
⚫ number strips on page 121

Preparing the centers:
1. Laminate the center mat and number strips.
2. Cut out the strips.
3. Cut slits in the center mat where indicated.
4. Place the programmed strips, center mat, and copies of the recording sheet at a center.

Using the centers:
1. A student inserts the strips into the corresponding slits in the center mat.
2. She slides the strip in Hive 1 to show problem A.
3. She slides the strip in Hive 2 to show the answer to problem A.
4. She completes the recording sheet on page 116.

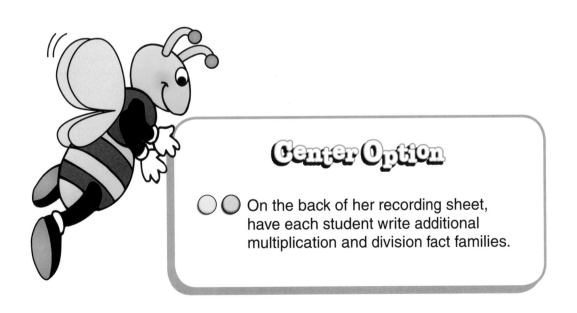

Center Option
⚪⚫ On the back of her recording sheet, have each student write additional multiplication and division fact families.

All Abuzz!

Color the circle to match your number strips. ◯

Copy problem A and its solution onto section A.
Write the other three number sentences in the fact family.
Continue in this same manner with the remaining problems.

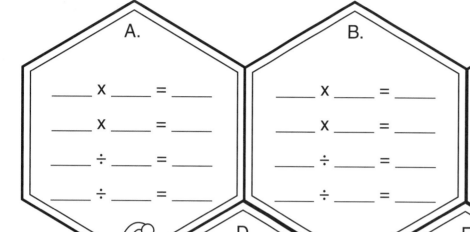

A.
___ x ___ = ___
___ x ___ = ___
___ ÷ ___ = ___
___ ÷ ___ = ___

B.
___ x ___ = ___
___ x ___ = ___
___ ÷ ___ = ___
___ ÷ ___ = ___

C.
___ x ___ = ___
___ x ___ = ___
___ ÷ ___ = ___
___ ÷ ___ = ___

D.
___ x ___ = ___
___ x ___ = ___
___ ÷ ___ = ___
___ ÷ ___ = ___

E.
___ x ___ = ___
___ x ___ = ___
___ ÷ ___ = ___
___ ÷ ___ = ___

F.
___ x ___ = ___
___ x ___ = ___
___ ÷ ___ = ___
___ ÷ ___ = ___

G.
___ x ___ = ___
___ x ___ = ___
___ ÷ ___ = ___
___ ÷ ___ = ___

H.
___ x ___ = ___
___ x ___ = ___
___ ÷ ___ = ___
___ ÷ ___ = ___

All Abuzz!

1. Insert the strips into the correct slits.
2. Slide the strip in Hive 1 to show problem A.
3. Slide the strip in Hive 2 to show the answer to problem A.
4. Complete page 116.

2

1

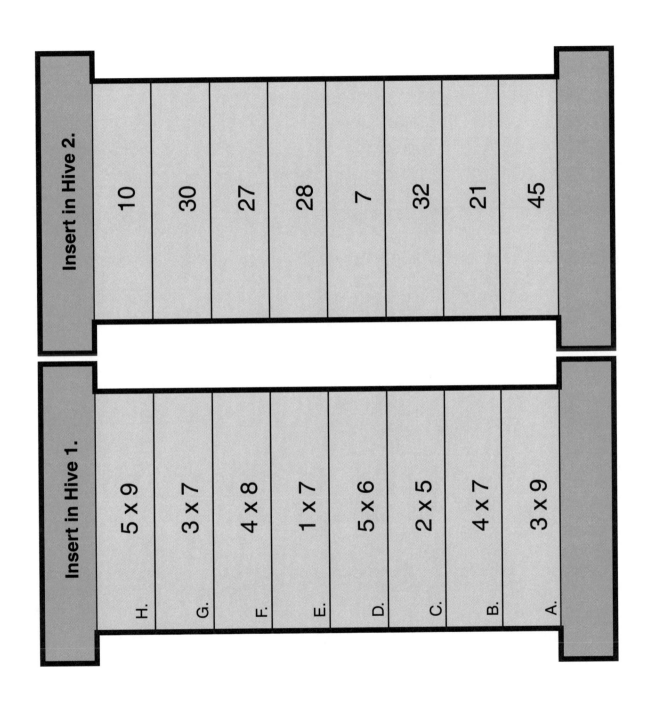

Insert in Hive 2.

| 10 |
| 30 |
| 27 |
| 28 |
| 7 |
| 32 |
| 21 |
| 45 |

Insert in Hive 1.

H.	5 x 9
G.	3 x 7
F.	4 x 8
E.	1 x 7
D.	5 x 6
C.	2 x 5
B.	4 x 7
A.	3 x 9

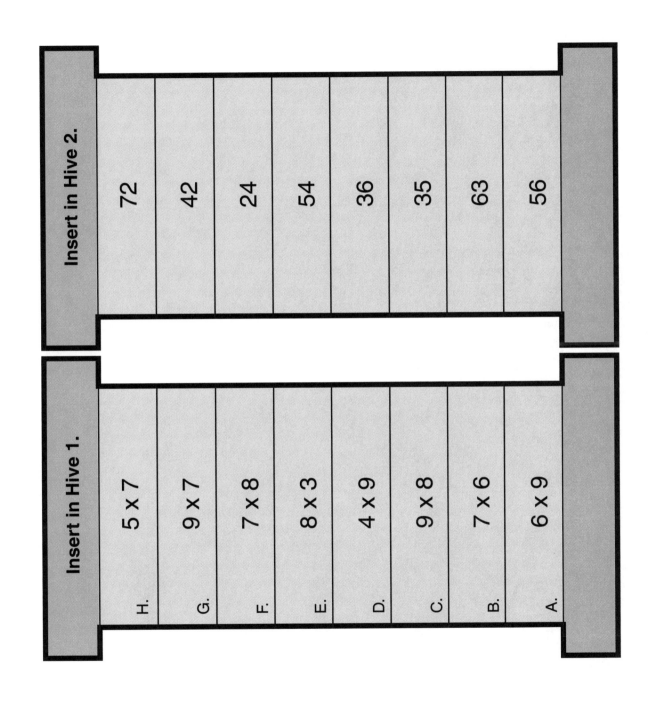

Insert in Hive 2.

| 72 | 42 | 24 | 54 | 36 | 35 | 63 | 56 |

Insert in Hive 1.

H.	G.	F.	E.	D.	C.	B.	A.
5 x 7	9 x 7	7 x 8	8 x 3	4 x 9	9 x 8	7 x 6	6 x 9

Music by Moonlight

 Multiplying without regrouping: 2 digits by 1 digit

 Multiplying without regrouping: 3 digits and 4 digits by 1 digit

Materials:
supply of the recording sheet on page 124
center mat on page 125
number wheels on page 127
number wheels on page 129
brad

Preparing the centers:
1. Laminate the center mat and wheels.
2. Cut out the wheels and the window in the center mat.
3. Poke a small hole through the black dot on each wheel and the center mat.
4. Place the programmed wheels, center mat, brad, and copies of the recording sheet at a center.

Using the centers:
1. A student uses the brad to attach the wheel to the back of the center mat.
2. She turns the wheel to show problem A.
3. She writes the problem and its answer on the recording sheet on page 124 beside its corresponding letter.
4. She continues in this same manner with the remaining problems.

Center Option
Program the open wheels with additional multiplication problems.

Name _____

Music by Moonlight

Color the circle to match the back of your number wheel. ◯

Copy problem A from the wheel onto tambourine A.
Multiply.
Continue in this same manner with the remaining problems.

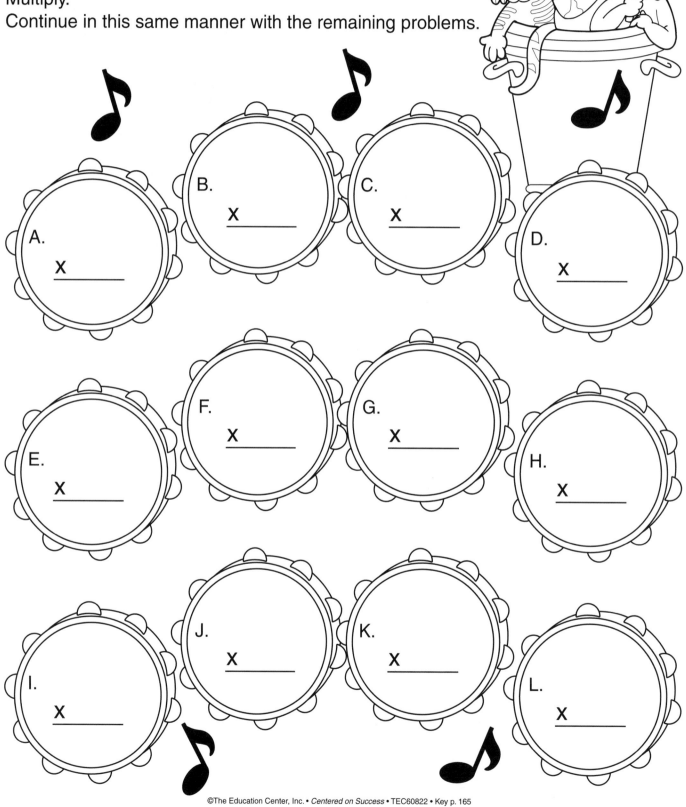

A.
   X ____

B.
   X ____

C.
   X ____

D.
   X ____

E.
   X ____

F.
   X ____

G.
   X ____

H.
   X ____

I.
   X ____

J.
   X ____

K.
   X ____

L.
   X ____

1. Attach the wheel to the back of this sheet with the brad.
2. Turn the wheel to show problem A.
3. Complete page 124.

Cut out.

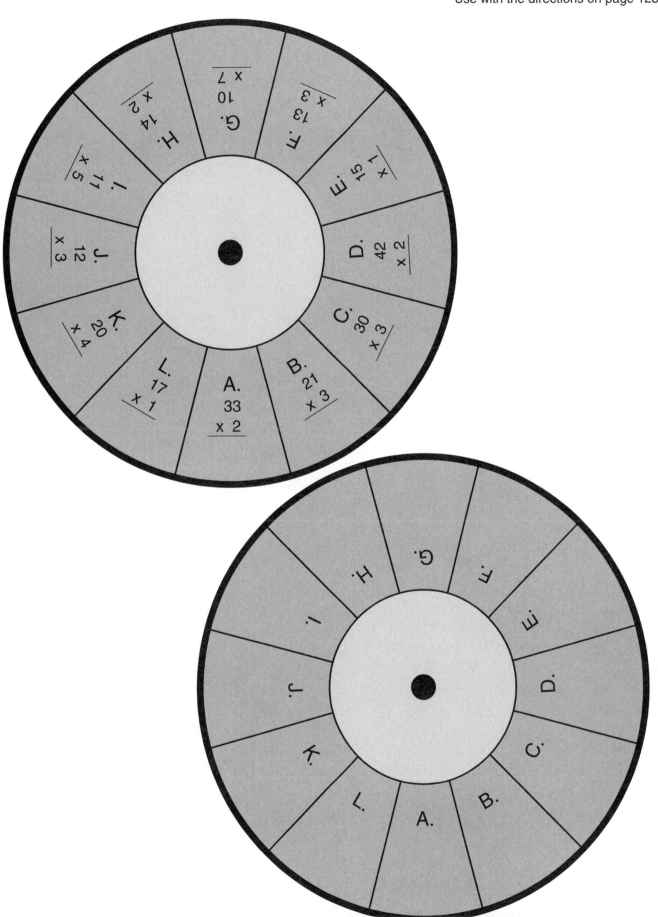

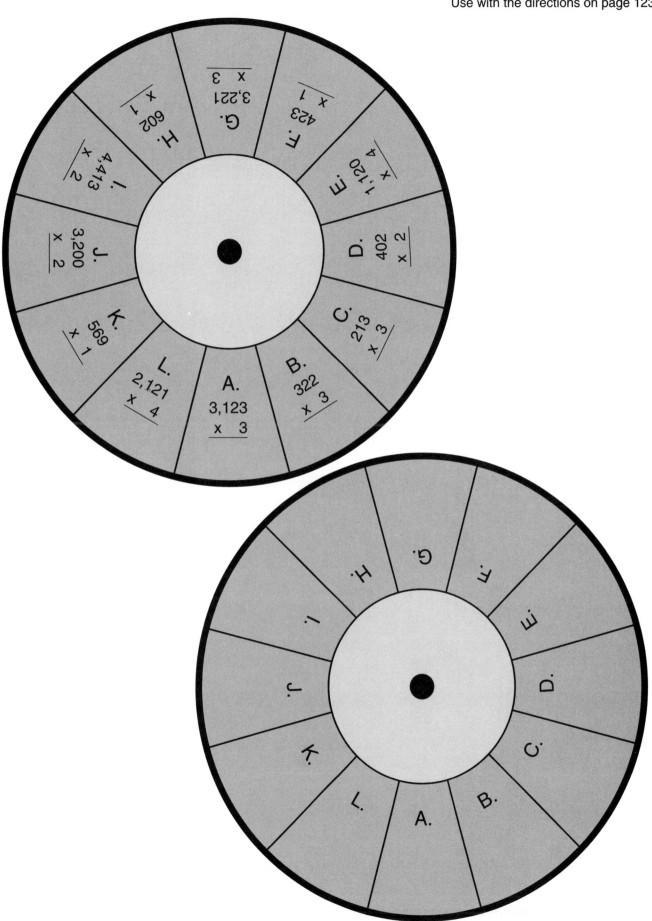

Up, Up, and Away!

 Multiplying with regrouping: 2 digits by 1 digit

 Multiplying with regrouping: 3 digits and 4 digits by 1 digit

Materials:
supply of the recording sheet on page 132
center mat on page 133
number strips on page 135
number strips on page 137

Preparing the centers:
1. Laminate the center mat and number strips.
2. Cut out the strips.
3. Cut slits in the center mat where indicated.
4. Place the center mat, programmed strips, and copies of the recording sheet at a center.

Using the centers:
1. A student inserts the strip into the slits in the center mat.
2. She slides the strip to show problem A.
3. She writes the problem and its answer on cloud A on the recording sheet on page 132.
4. She continues in this same manner with the remaining problems.

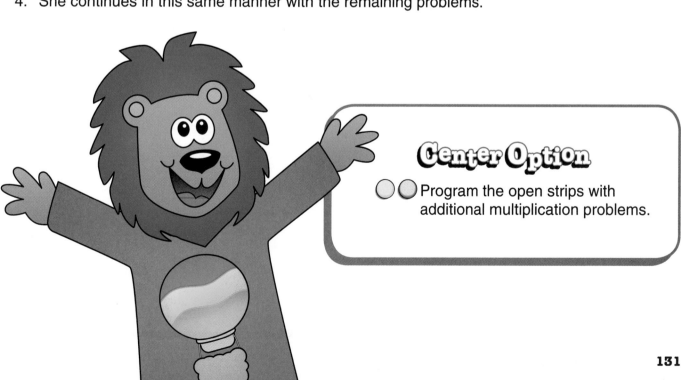

Center Option
Program the open strips with additional multiplication problems.

Up, Up, and Away!

Color the circle to match the back of your number strip.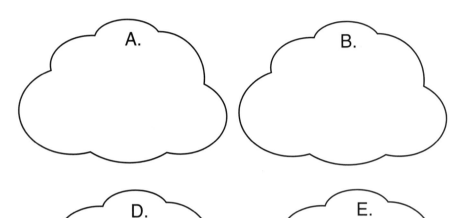

Copy problem A from the strip onto cloud A.
Write the correct answer.
Continue in this same manner with the remaining problems.

A.

B.

C.

D.

E.

F.

G.

H.

I.

J.

K.

L.

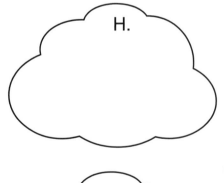

©The Education Center, Inc. • *Centered on Success* • TEC60822 • Key p. 165

132 **Note to the teacher:** Use with the directions on page 131.

Up, Up, and Away!

1. Insert the strip into the slits.
2. Slide the strip to show problem A.
3. Complete page 132.

L.	41 x 9 =
K.	27 x 3 =
J.	65 x 4 =
I.	54 x 5 =
H.	18 x 4 =
G.	12 x 8 =
F.	72 x 6 =
E.	15 x 2 =
D.	24 x 7 =
C.	33 x 6 =
B.	52 x 5 =
A.	48 x 3 =

L.	
K.	
J.	
I.	
H.	
G.	
F.	
E.	
D.	
C.	
B.	
A.	

Number Strips

Use with the directions on page 131.

L.	2,600 x 3 =
K.	582 x 5 =
J.	1,350 x 4 =
I.	624 x 2 =
H.	2,361 x 7 =
G.	412 x 9 =
F.	219 x 6 =
E.	1,703 x 8 =
D.	106 x 4 =
C.	1,217 x 5 =
B.	426 x 2 =
A.	3,521 x 3 =

L.
K.
J.
I.
H.
G.
F.
E.
D.
C.
B.
A.

High-Jumping Hippos

 Identifying information on a bar graph

 Interpreting and comparing information on a bar graph

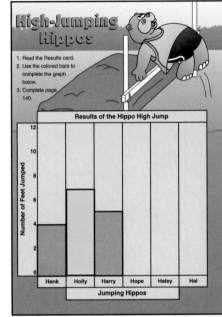

Materials:
supply of the recording sheet on page 140
center mat on page 141
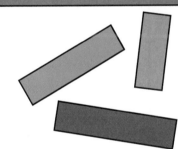 cards and colored bars on page 143
cards and colored bars on page 145
2 resealable plastic bags

Preparing the centers:
1. Laminate the center mat, cards, and colored bars if desired.
2. Cut apart the cards and bars and put each set into a separate bag.
3. Place the bags, center mat, and copies of the recording sheet at a center.

Using the centers:
1. A student removes the cards and colored bars from the bag.
2. He reads the information on the results card.
3. He uses the bars to complete the graph.
4. He completes the recording sheet on page 140.

Center Option
Invite pairs to complete the center together. Have students take turns reading a sentence from the results card and correctly placing the bars to complete the graph.

High-Jumping Hippos

Color the circle to match the back of your center cards. ◯

Label and draw your completed graph below.

| 12 |
| 10 |
| 8 |
| 6 |
| 4 |
| 2 |
| 0 |

Read each sentence on the Questions card.

Write each answer below.

A. _____ B. _____ C. _____

D. _____ E. _____ F. _____

High-Jumping Hippos

1. Read the Results card.
2. Use the colored bars to complete the graph below.
3. Complete page 140.

Results of the Hippo High Jump

Number of Feet Jumped

12

10

8

6

4

2

0

| Hank | Holly | Harry | Hope | Haley | Hal |

Jumping Hippos

High Jump Results

Hal jumped 6 feet.

Harry jumped 5 feet.

Hank jumped 4 feet.

Hope jumped 10 feet.

Haley jumped 9 feet.

Holly jumped 7 feet.

Questions

A. How many hippos jumped?

B. How high did Hal jump?

C. Who jumped 9 feet?

D. How high did Harry jump?

E. Who jumped 7 feet?

F. Who jumped the highest?

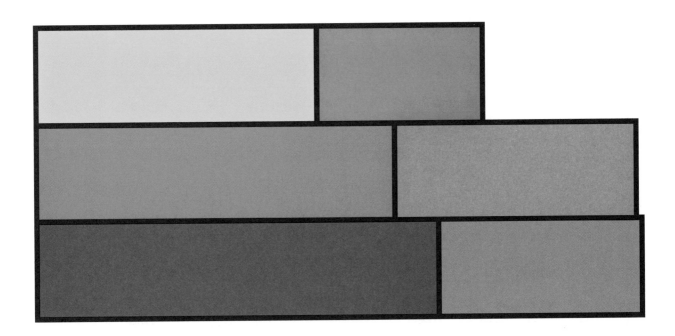

High Jump Results

Hope jumped 3 feet.

Harry jumped 8 feet.

Hank jumped 2 feet.

Haley jumped 11 feet.

Holly jumped 12 feet.

Hal jumped 5 feet.

Questions

A. How high did Harry jump?

B. How much higher did Haley jump than Hal?

C. How much higher did Harry jump than Hank?

D. How high did Holly and Hope jump together?

E. How high did Haley and Hank jump together?

F. How high did the hippos jump all together?

Something's Fishy!

 Identifying appropriate units of measure: inches, feet, miles

 Identifying appropriate units of measure: centimeters, meters, inches, feet, miles

Materials:
supply of the recording sheet on page 148
center mat on page 149
○ sentence strips on page 151
○ sentence strips on page 153

Preparing the centers:
1. Laminate the center mat and sentence strips.
2. Cut out the strips.
3. Cut slits in the center mat where indicated.
4. Place the programmed strips, center mat, and copies of the recording sheet at a center.

Using the centers:
1. A student inserts the strip into the slits in the center mat.
2. She slides the strip to show problem A.
3. She writes the complete sentence on the recording sheet on page 148 next to the corresponding letter.
4. She continues in this same manner with the remaining sentences.

Center Option
○ ○ Program the open strips with additional incomplete sentences.

Something's Fishy!

Color the circle to match the back of your ○ sentence strip.

Read problem A and decide which unit of measure should be used.
Write the complete sentence on Line A.
Continue in this same manner with the remaining sentences.

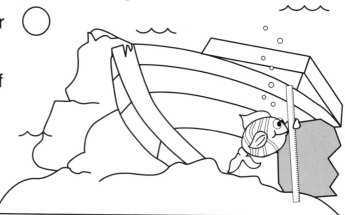

A. _____

B. _____

C. _____

D. _____

E. _____

F. _____

G. _____

H. _____

I. _____

J. _____

Something's Fishy!

1. Insert the strip into the slits.
2. Slide the strip to show problem A.
3. Complete page 148.

J. My hand is about 3 _____ wide.

  feet   inches

I. Notebook paper is about 1 _____ long.

  foot   inch

H. The school is 2 _____ from my house.

  miles   feet

G. A paper clip is about 1 _____ long.

  inch   foot

F. The next town is 6 _____ away.

  feet   miles

E. My desk is 24 _____ wide.

  inches   feet

D. My sister is 3 _____ tall.

  feet   inches

C. The ceiling is 9 _____ high.

  inches   feet

B. We drove 3 _____ to the mall.

  feet   miles

A. The crayon is 3 _____ long.

  inches   feet

J.

I.

H.

G.

F.

E.

D.

C.

B.

A.

J. The chair is about 1 _____ tall.
    meter   inch

I. He walked 1 _____ in 20 minutes.
    yard   mile

H. My arm span is about 1 _____ wide.
    meter   foot

G. A glue stick is about 8 _____ long.
    centimeters   inches

F. A car is about 3 _____ long.
    meters   miles

E. The store is 4 _____ from my house.
    feet   miles

D. She ran 400 _____ in 7 minutes.
    centimeters   meters

C. A key is about 2 _____ long.
    centimeters   inches

B. One lap around the school is 1,000 _____.
    meters   miles

A. My thumb is about 4 _____ long.
    inches   centimeters

J.

I.

H.

G.

F.

E.

D.

C.

B.

A.

Croc's Cool Clock

 Telling time: half hour, quarter hour

 Telling time: quarter hour, 5 minutes

Materials:
supply of the recording sheet on page 156
center mat on page 157
⬤ time cards on page 159
⬤ time cards on page 161
2 resealable plastic bags
brad

Preparing the centers:
1. Laminate the center mat, time cards, and clock hands if desired.
2. Cut out the cards and clock hands and put each programmed set into a separate bag.
3. Poke the brad through the long clock hand, the short clock hand, and the clockface on the center mat (in that order); then fasten the brad.
4. Place the bags, center mat, and copies of the recording sheet at a center.

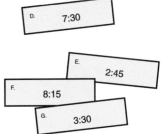

Using the centers:
1. A student removes the time cards from the bag and stacks them in order with card A on top.
2. He selects card A, reads the time, and lays it on the center sheet where indicated.
3. He moves the clock hands to show the time.
4. He draws the clock hands on the recording sheet on page 156 to match.
5. He writes the time on the lines below the clock.
6. He continues in this same manner with the remaining cards.

Center Option
⬤⬤ Program the open cards with additional times.

Croc's Cool Clock

Color the circle to match the back of your time cards. ◯

Draw clock hands to show the time on card A.
Write the time below clock A.
Continue in this same manner with the remaining cards.

A. _____ : _____

B. _____ : _____

C. _____ : _____

D. _____ : _____

E. _____ : _____

F. _____ : _____

G. _____ : _____

H. _____ : _____

I. _____ : _____

Croc's Cool Clock

1. Select card A and read it.
2. Lay the card on the crate.
3. Use the clock hands to show the time.
4. Complete page 156.

Place card here.

A. **6:30**	A. **:**
B. **5:45**	B. **:**
C. **10:15**	C. **:**
D. **7:30**	D. **:**
E. **2:45**	E. **:**
F. **8:15**	F. **:**
G. **3:30**	G. **:**
H. **1:45**	H. **:**
I. **12:15**	I. **:**

hour hand   **minute hand**

A. **2:35**	A. **:**
B. **6:55**	B. **:**
C. **7:45**	C. **:**
D. **5:40**	D. **:**
E. **12:05**	E. **:**
F. **4:15**	F. **:**
G. **10:25**	G. **:**
H. **3:35**	H. **:**
I. **1:45**	I. **:**

Answer Keys

Page 4 (Y)

ai	igh
brain	sight
pain	tight
paint	bright
wait	might

a-e	i-e
take	spice
shake	rise
space	pride
bake	mile

ay	y
play	sly
stray	try
way	why
may	my

Page 4 (B)

ai	igh
snail	light
tail	knight
rain	night
chain	thigh

a-e	i-e
whale	knife
lace	kite
gate	mice
scale	fire

ay	y
tray	fly
crayon	sky
hay	cry
spray	fry

Page 12 (Y)

unfair—not fair
unhappy—not happy
untrue—not true
unprepared—not prepared
unsure—not sure
retest—test again
redraw—draw again
rewrite—write again
retry—try again
reread—read again

Page 12 (B)

prepay—pay before
preview—view before
preheat—heat before
preset—set before
prewash—wash before
mismatch—mix up
mistreat—treat poorly
misspell—spell incorrectly
misplace—to lose
misbehave—behave poorly

Page 20 (Y)

1. Sammy ate his dinner quickly.
2. Sally was careful on the stage.
3. The seals rested quietly after dinner.
4. Scott hit the ball softly to Sammy.
5. Eating fish makes the seals cheerful.
6. Sally and Scott are very playful after lunch.
7. The seals' mother tries to be helpful.
8. All the seals swim slowly after they eat.
9. Sammy likes to play with colorful balls.
10. The seals wait calmly for their dinner each night.

Page 20 (B)

1. Sally is warmer in the sun than in the water.
2. Of all the seals, Sammy is the loudest.
3. Scott's teeth are the cleanest in the family.
4. Scott is older than Sally.
5. The seals think they are the smartest animals.
6. Sally's ball is newer than Sammy's.
7. The seals' mother's stage is the tallest.
8. Sally's flippers are shorter than Scott's.
9. Sammy can balance a ball longer than Sally.
10. Juggling five balls is harder than juggling three.

Page 28 (Y)

1. cake
   gifts
   balloons
   Birthday Items
2. terrier
   spaniel
   poodle
   Dogs
3. parent
   sister
   uncle
   Relatives
4. hockey
   tennis
   soccer
   Sports
5. red
   green
   orange
   Colors
6. bagel
   pickle
   cracker
   Foods
7. pants
   shirt
   shorts
   Clothes
8. soda
   coffee
   juice
   Drinks

Page 28 (B)

1. soap
   washcloth
   sponge
   Cleaning Items
2. notebook
   desk
   test
   School Items
3. wagon
   bike
   car
   Things With Wheels
4. whistle
   siren
   horn
   Noisy Things
5. clock
   ruler
   scale
   Things That Measure
6. fireworks
   play
   movie
   Things to Watch
7. hill
   valley
   mountain
   Landforms
8. globe
   wheel
   golf ball
   Round Things

Page 36 (Y)

Facts
Crayons come in different colors.
Crayons can melt.
Crayons are made of wax.
Crayons can break.
Crayons come in different sizes.

Opinions
There is nothing better than a sharp crayon.
The prettiest crayon of all is blue.
It is really fun to draw with crayons.
Crayons are much better than markers.
All crayons smell great!

Page 36 (B)

Facts
All crayons are made of wax.
You can buy crayons at the store.
There are violet and pink crayons.
Crayola crayons were first made in 1903.
Some crayons are dark.

Opinions
Crayons are not messy.
Crayons have a nice smell.
The red crayon is pretty.
Sharp crayons are the best.
Drawing with crayons is fun.

Page 44 Ⓨ

Is this a large desert?
A cactus can store its own water.
Why does a cactus have sharp spines?
Many different kinds of animals live in the desert.
The desert can get very cold at night.
There is not much water in the desert.
Is the desert flat or hilly?
I would like to have a cactus of my own.

Page 44 Ⓑ

I had a cactus. Do you know where it is?
Temperatures in the desert can reach 107°F. Wow, that's really hot!
Can you grow your own cactus? How do you do it?
I'd like to visit the desert someday. When can we go?
Wow, this is beautiful! It reminds me of home.
There are many spiders living in the desert. Some are very large.
This desert is very flat. Do you know where we are?
Would you like to visit the desert someday? Sure!

Page 52 Ⓨ

1. The Ants went to the beach on May 29, 2002.
2. Annie Ant visited Lincoln, Nebraska, last month.
3. The Ant family lives in Richmond, Virginia.
4. Annie started Ant School on August 28, 1999.
5. Alex Ant was born on September 23, 2000.
6. Ada Ant moved to Miami, Florida, last year.
7. Ada and Annie went to a picnic on July 4, 2002.
8. The Ant family reunion was June 15, 2003.
9. Annie lives in Spokane, Washington.
10. Ada was born on March 26, 2001.

Page 52 Ⓑ

1. Annie Ant loves pizza, potato chips, and chocolate.
2. The Ants might move to Detroit, Michigan.
3. Alex Ant took a train to Sacramento, California.
4. The world's largest picnic is in Chicago, Illinois.
5. Ada Ant needed paper, pencils, and glue for school.
6. The museum is in Santa Fe, New Mexico.
7. The Ant family visited Raleigh, North Carolina.
8. Ada bought pants, shoes, and socks for the trip.
9. Annie bought ice cream, milk, and bread at the store.
10. Alex lives in Atlanta, Georgia.

Page 60 Ⓨ

Monday
July
February
June
September
Wednesday
Kwanzaa
Flag Day

Page 60 Ⓑ

Dover Drive
Ann's Gift Shop
State Street
Bramble Bakery
The Happy Hotel
Sugar Creek
Old Village School
Pine Point Park

Page 68 Ⓨ

was not—wasn't
have not—haven't
that is—that's
it is—it's
can not—can't
he is—he's
are not—aren't
she is—she's
do not—don't

Page 68 Ⓑ

will not—won't
we have—we've
could not—couldn't
I will—I'll
does not—doesn't
you have—you've
they will—they'll
I have—I've
you will—you'll

Page 76 Ⓨ

(Answers may vary.)
Nouns
frogs
leaf
legs
grass

Verbs
sleeping
wiggle
eat
sits

Other
of
loudly
the
big

Page 76 Ⓑ

(Answers may vary.)
Nouns
pond
legs
friend
pebble

Verbs
jumping
diving
see
swims

Adjectives
small
funny
bumpy
happy

Page 84 Ⓨ

A. 214 < 241
B. 301 > 299
C. 712 < 721
D. 961 > 691
E. 999 > 991
F. 764 > 674
G. 892 > 891
H. 301 < 310
I. 202 < 220
J. 546 < 564
K. 476 > 467
L. 633 > 631

Page 84 Ⓑ

A. 7,999 < 8,000
B. 6,350 < 6,560
C. 9,911 > 9,199
D. 5,425 > 4,525
E. 2,001 < 2,100
F. 1,358 > 1,357
G. 7,403 > 7,304
H. 8,500 > 8,150
I. 6,162 < 6,261
J. 9,212 > 9,121
K. 5,297 < 5,710
L. 8,000 < 8,888

Page 92 Ⓨ

A. 4 x 6 = 24
B. 3 x 4 = 12
C. 2 x 5 = 10
D. 4 x 8 = 32
E. 3 x 3 = 9
F. 2 x 6 = 12
G. 1 x 9 = 9
H. 2 x 2 = 4
I. 4 x 9 = 36
J. 3 x 5 = 15
K. 4 x 4 = 16
L. 3 x 7 = 21

Page 92 Ⓑ

A. 6 x 5 = 30
B. 5 x 7 = 35
C. 4 x 8 = 32
D. 3 x 9 = 27
E. 4 x 5 = 20
F. 5 x 8 = 40
G. 6 x 7 = 42
H. 6 x 9 = 54
I. 4 x 9 = 36
J. 5 x 4 = 20
K. 3 x 6 = 18
L. 6 x 8 = 48

Page 100 Ⓨ
Answers will vary.

Page 100 Ⓑ
Answers will vary.

Page 124 Ⓨ
A. 33 x 2 = 66
B. 21 x 3 = 63
C. 30 x 3 = 90
D. 42 x 2 = 84
E. 15 x 1 = 15
F. 13 x 3 = 39
G. 10 x 7 = 70
H. 14 x 2 = 28
I. 11 x 5 = 55
J. 12 x 3 = 36
K. 20 x 4 = 80
L. 17 x 1 = 17

Page 124 Ⓑ
A. 3,123 x 3 = 9,369
B. 322 x 3 = 966
C. 213 x 3 = 639
D. 402 x 2 = 804
E. 1,120 x 4 = 4,480
F. 423 x 1 = 423
G. 3,221 x 3 = 9,663
H. 602 x 1 = 602
I. 4,413 x 2 = 8,826
J. 3,200 x 2 = 6,400
K. 569 x 1 = 569
L. 2,121 x 4 = 8,484

Page 108 Ⓨ
8 x 7 = 56
7 x 5 = 35
8 x 9 = 72
7 x 7 = 49
4 x 9 = 36
3 x 5 = 15
6 x 9 = 54
3 x 9 = 27
2 x 9 = 18
8 x 3 = 24
8 x 8 = 64
8 x 4 = 32

Page 108 Ⓑ
10 x 8 = 80
9 x 5 = 45
10 x 2 = 20
9 x 9 = 81
10 x 3 = 30
8 x 7 = 56
10 x 9 = 90
8 x 6 = 48
10 x 7 = 70
10 x 6 = 60
9 x 7 = 63
10 x 5 = 50

Page 132 Ⓨ
A. 48 x 3 = 144
B. 52 x 5 = 260
C. 33 x 6 = 198
D. 24 x 7 =168
E. 15 x 2 = 30
F. 72 x 6 = 432
G. 12 x 8 = 96
H. 18 x 4 = 72
I. 54 x 5 = 270
J. 65 x 4 = 260
K. 27 x 3 = 81
L. 41 x 9 = 369

Page 132 Ⓑ
A. 3,521 x 3 = 10,563
B. 426 x 2 = 852
C. 1,217 x 5 = 6,085
D. 106 x 4 = 424
E. 1,703 x 8 = 13,624
F. 219 x 6 = 1,314
G. 412 x 9 = 3,708
H. 2,361 x 7 = 16,527
I. 624 x 2 = 1,248
J. 1,350 x 4 = 5,400
K. 582 x 5 = 2,910
L. 2,600 x 3 = 7,800

Page 116 Ⓨ
A. 3 x 9 = 27
   9 x 3 = 27
   27 ÷ 3 = 9
   27 ÷ 9 = 3

B. 4 x 7 = 28
   7 x 4 = 28
   28 ÷ 4 = 7
   28 ÷ 7 = 4

C. 2 x 5 = 10
   5 x 2 = 10
   10 ÷ 2 = 5
   10 ÷ 5 = 2

D. 5 x 6 = 30
   6 x 5 = 30
   30 ÷ 5 = 6
   30 ÷ 6 = 5

E. 1 x 7 = 7
   7 x 1 = 7
   7 ÷ 1 = 7
   7 ÷ 7 = 1

F. 4 x 8 = 32
   8 x 4 = 32
   32 ÷ 4 = 8
   32 ÷ 8 = 4

G. 3 x 7 = 21
   7 x 3 = 21
   21 ÷ 3 = 7
   21 ÷ 7 = 3

H. 5 x 9 = 45
   9 x 5 = 45
   45 ÷ 5 = 9
   45 ÷ 9 = 5

Page 116 Ⓑ
A. 6 x 9 = 54
   9 x 6 = 54
   54 ÷ 6 = 9
   54 ÷ 9 = 6

B. 7 x 6 = 42
   6 x 7 = 42
   42 ÷ 7 = 6
   42 ÷ 6 = 7

C. 9 x 8 = 72
   8 x 9 = 72
   72 ÷ 9 = 8
   72 ÷ 8 = 9

D. 4 x 9 = 36
   9 x 4 = 36
   36 ÷ 4 = 9
   36 ÷ 9 = 4

E. 8 x 3 = 24
   3 x 8 = 24
   24 ÷ 8 = 3
   24 ÷ 3 = 8

F. 7 x 8 = 56
   8 x 7 = 56
   56 ÷ 7 = 8
   56 ÷ 8 = 7

G. 9 x 7 = 63
   7 x 9 = 63
   63 ÷ 9 = 7
   63 ÷ 7 = 9

H. 5 x 7 = 35
   7 x 5 = 35
   35 ÷ 5 = 7
   35 ÷ 7 = 5

Page 140 Ⓨ
A. 6 hippos
B. 6 feet
C. Haley
D. 5 feet
E. Holly
F. Hope

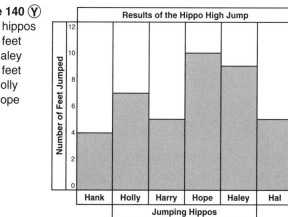

Page 140 Ⓑ
A. 8 feet
B. 6 feet
C. 6 feet
D. 15 feet
E. 13 feet
F. 41 feet

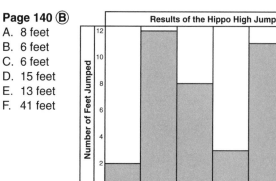

Page 148 Ⓨ

A. The crayon is 3 inches long.
B. We drove 3 miles to the mall.
C. The ceiling is 9 feet high.
D. My sister is 3 feet tall.
E. My desk is 24 inches wide.
F. The next town is 6 miles away.
G. A paper clip is about 1 inch long.
H. The school is 2 miles from my house.
I. Notebook paper is about 1 foot long.
J. My hand is about 3 inches wide.

Page 148 Ⓑ

A. My thumb is about 4 centimeters long.
B. One lap around the school is 1,000 meters.
C. A key is about 2 inches long.
D. She ran 400 meters in 7 minutes.
E. The store is 4 miles from my house.
F. A car is about 3 meters long.
G. A glue stick is about 8 centimeters long.
H. My arm span is about 1 meter wide.
I. He walked 1 mile in 20 minutes.
J. The chair is about 1 meter tall.

Page 156 Ⓨ

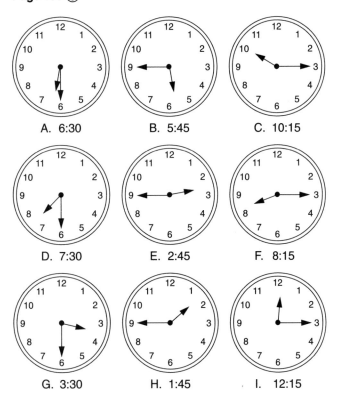

A. 6:30   B. 5:45   C. 10:15

D. 7:30   E. 2:45   F. 8:15

G. 3:30   H. 1:45   I. 12:15

Page 156 Ⓑ

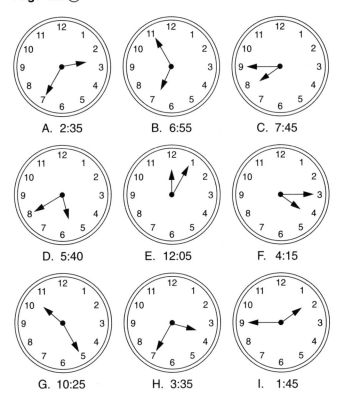

A. 2:35   B. 6:55   C. 7:45

D. 5:40   E. 12:05   F. 4:15

G. 10:25   H. 3:35   I. 1:45